HUMMINGBIRDS

by Bonnie Bader

Grosset & Dunlap
An Imprint of Penguin Group (USA) LLC

For Mom, who is always fluttering in my thoughts—BB

GROSSET & DUNLAP
Published by the Penguin Group
Penguin Group (USA) LLC, 375 Hudson Street, New York, New York 10014, USA

USA | Canada | UK | Ireland | Australia | New Zealand | India | South Africa | China

penguin.com
A Penguin Random House Company

Photo credits: cover, back cover, title page: © Thinkstock/drferry; page 3: © Thinkstock/Altin Osmanaj;
page 4: © Thinkstock/gualbertobecerra; pages 5, 6, 7, 8, 21: (cloud) © Thinkstock/Faruk SISKO;
page 5: (map) © Thinkstock/Mastamak; page 6: (bird and flower) © Thinkstock/Richard Rodvold,
(Alaska) © Thinkstock/AlexanderZam; page 7: (bird and flower) © Thinkstock/Ivan Paunovic, (Chile) ©
Thinkstock/PeterHermesFurian; page 8: (bird) © Thinkstock/gualbertobecerra, (Ecuador) © Thinkstock/
PeterHermesFurian; page 9: (bird) © Thinkstock/Bob Balestri, (Cuba) © Thinkstock/PeterHermesFurian;
page 10: (small bird) © Thinkstock/natureniche, (large bird) © Thinkstock/gatito33; page 11: © Thinkstock/
André Schäfer; page 12: © Thinkstock/Thomas Koellner; page 13: © Thinkstock/Katrina Brown; page 14: ©
Thinkstock/Rainbohm; page 15: © Getty/Carl Jackson Photography; page 16: © Thinkstock/Haydoce; page 17: ©
Thinkstock/Rob Stegmann; pages 18–19: © Thinkstock/kwantse; page 20: © Thinkstock/Todd Taulman;
page 21: © Thinkstock/Steve Byland; page 22: © Thinkstock/Michael & Patricia Fogden; page 23: © Thinkstock/
TylerFairbank; page 24: © Thinkstock/PCHT; page 25: © Thinkstock/Dennis Donohue; pages 26–27: ©
Thinkstock/kwantse; page 28: © Thinkstock/billberryphotography; page 29: © Thinkstock/Bkamprath;
page 30: © Thinkstock/phakimata; page 31: © Thinkstock/kojihirano; page 32: © Thinkstock/IccPortillo.

Library of Congress Cataloging-in-Publication Data is available.

ISBN 978-0-448-48713-7 (pbk)   10 9 8 7 6 5 4 3
ISBN 978-0-448-48714-4 (hc)   10 9 8 7 6 5 4 3 2 1

Something is flittering.
Something is fluttering.
What do you see?

It's a hummingbird, the smallest bird in the world!

There are more than 320 different species, or kinds, of hummingbirds. But they only live in parts of the Western Hemisphere. The Western Hemisphere is the half of the world that includes North and South America.

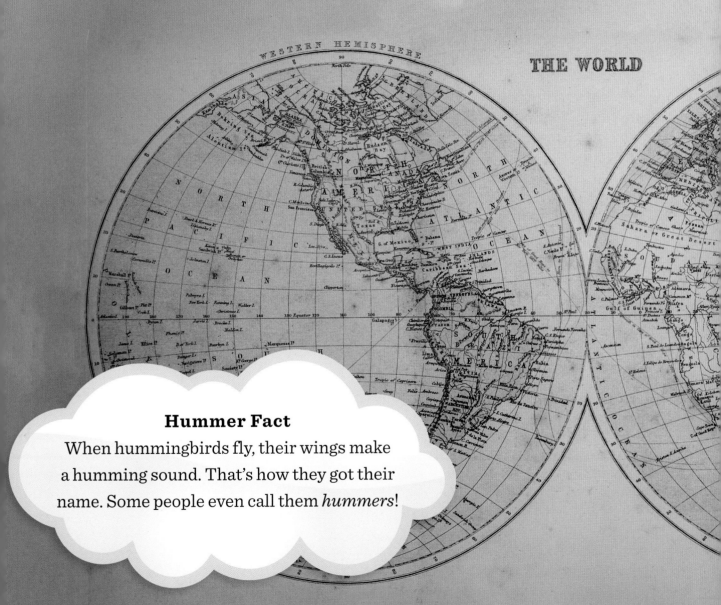

Hummer Fact

When hummingbirds fly, their wings make a humming sound. That's how they got their name. Some people even call them *hummers*!

Some, like the rufous hummingbird, live as far north as Alaska.

ALASKA

Hummer Fact
In the winter, the rufous hummingbird migrates, or flies, to Mexico. Once, scientists put a band on a rufous hummingbird to track how far it would fly during migration. They were amazed to find out that this little hummingbird flew about 3,500 miles from Florida to Alaska!

Other hummingbirds, like the Chilean woodstar, live as far south as Chile.

Hummer Fact
The Chilean woodstar is endangered, because many of the plants it feeds on have been destroyed. Without these plants, the Chilean woodstar population has begun to die out.

BOLIVIA

PARAGUAY

CHILE

URUGUAY

PACIFIC OCEAN

ARGENTINA

The largest hummingbird in the world, the giant hummingbird, can be found in South America. But this bird isn't really giant—it's only eight inches long!

COLOMBIA

ECUADOR

BRAZIL

PERU

PACIFIC OCEAN

BOLI

Hummer Fact
Ecuador has the widest variety of hummingbird species—around 150 different kinds of hummingbirds live there!

CUBA

Cayman Islands

HAITI

JAMAICA

DOMINICAN
REPUBLIC

C A R I B B E A N   S E A

The tiniest hummingbird
lives in Cuba.
The bee hummingbird is
only about two inches long!

Hummingbirds such as the broad-tailed
and the calliope can be found in the United States.
But no matter where you are, you need to have
good eyesight to spot a hummingbird!

What is that spot of white?
Is it a pearl?
Is it a jelly bean?

ACTUAL SIZE

No, it's a
hummingbird egg!

Hummingbirds lay the smallest eggs of all birds.

They are less than half an inch long.

Shake, shake!

Wiggle, wiggle!

The mother hummingbird has laid a second egg.

The eggs take between fifteen and twenty days to hatch.
The mother keeps the eggs safe in a nest.
Before she laid her eggs, the mother built the nest all by herself.

The father did not help.
The mother used twigs,
leaves, moss, lichen, feathers, and
spiderweb silk to make her nest.

Inside the eggs, the
babies peck their way out.
Peck, peck, peck!

Out come the babies.
They have no feathers.
Their skin is dark.
And they are tiny. Each one
weighs less than a dime!

Watch out! Sometimes larger animals, such as blue jays or hawks, swoop down into the nest and eat the chicks. The mother will protect her chicks from predators with loud, fast-paced chirping, sharp diving, and fighting using her needlelike bill.

Adult hummingbirds are fast. If attacked, they can escape from most predators.

The mother has to sit on the chicks to keep them warm.
The only time she leaves the nest is to find food.

Hummingbirds get their food from flowers.
But it's not the sweet smell from the flowers that attracts these little birds. It's the bright colors—orange, red, and purple.

A hummingbird uses its special tongue to get nectar, a sweet liquid, from the flowers.

Its tongue is shaped like a little fork with fringes on the edges.

This helps the hummingbird lick up the nectar.

A hummingbird does more than get nectar from flowers. It helps with pollination! Pollination occurs when a fine powder called pollen is transferred from one part of a flower to another. This causes plants to make seeds. And seeds are needed to make new flowers. Plants cannot make seeds unless they are pollinated.

When a hummingbird sticks its head into a long, trumpet-shaped flower, some of the pollen sticks to its head and body. The hummingbird carries this pollen with it from flower to flower.

If it weren't for hummingbirds, many flowers wouldn't exist!

Some hummingbirds' bills fit exactly into the flowers they feed from, like two pieces of a puzzle!
The white-tipped sicklebill hummingbird has a very curvy beak. It might look strange, but it's a perfect fit for the heliconia flower.

Hummingbirds also eat small insects and spiders.
Swoop! The mother hummingbird darts down.

The mother flies back to her nest.

Whoosh! The baby birds feel the wind from their mother's wings. They tip up their heads and open their mouths.

The mother throws up the food into her mouth. The food is now liquid and soft—a perfect meal for the babies!

She puts her beak inside the babies' mouths and drops in the food. She has to feed her babies once every twenty minutes to keep them healthy!

All hummingbirds, not only the babies, need to eat a lot. Each day, hummingbirds eat up to three times their weight in sugar and protein. Some hummingbirds even eat eight times their weight! This is because they burn so much energy. Their hearts beat as many as 1,200 times per minute! Hummingbirds visit thousands of flowers each day just to stay alive.

The hummingbird flies out to find more food. She hovers over a flower. It may look like she is staying still, but she is actually beating her wings very fast. Some hummingbirds can beat their wings as fast as two hundred times per second.

Hummingbirds are the only birds that fly forward, backward, sideways, and upside down.

And even though hummingbirds have feet, most of them can't walk. They use their feet for perching.

What's that flash of emerald?
It's the baby hummingbirds!

Three weeks have passed. They have left the nest. Now they are looking for food, just like their mother. As they fly, hummingbirds' feathers shine in the light.

Hummingbird feathers are iridescent. The feathers look like they are glittering in the light. Most male hummingbirds have bright, shiny feathers. The female hummingbirds have duller-colored feathers.

It is nighttime.

The hummingbird goes to sleep.

Its sleep, called *torpor*, is very deep. It is almost like it is in hibernation.

Its heart rate slows down.

Its breathing steadies.

The hummingbird is saving a lot of energy.

The next day, the sun rises.
It is time for the hummingbird
to wake up. And flit and flutter
to the flowers once more.